Original title:
Ripples of the Reef

Copyright © 2025 Creative Arts Management OÜ
All rights reserved.

Author: Kieran Blackwood
ISBN HARDBACK: 978-1-80587-312-9
ISBN PAPERBACK: 978-1-80587-782-0

Moondance on Aquatic Canvases

Under the moon, fish flash and sway,
Doing a jig in their watery ballet.
A crab joins in, clicks his claws,
While seaweed sways, whispering 'Applause!'

Starfish winks, they're quite the scene,
Mermaids giggle, keeping it clean.
The octopus twirls, ink in the air,
While turtles watch, but don't really care.

Pulse of the Oceanic Heart

Bubbles pop as a dolphin grins,
He's got moves, like disco spins.
A sea lion barks, 'Join the fun!'
While clams clap shells, thinking they've won.

The pufferfish puffs, what a trick,
A jellyfish jives, oh so slick.
With each wave, they dance with glee,
Together they form a wavy marquee.

Murmurs from the Abyss

Down in the gloom, a snail spins tales,
Of pirates, treasure, and sea monster scales.
His friends all chuckle—oh, what a jest,
While anglerfish grins, really impressed.

The octopus lounges, sipping his brew,
Says, "Hey, a bubble! Let's pop a few!"
Even the deep-sea fish can't resist,
As laughter echoes through the dark mist.

Tidal Tales of the Mystics

From the shore, crabs tell some wise cracking lore,
About mermaids who play "Hide and Seek" on the floor.
A shark shakes its head, 'Not on my shift!'
As the seashells giggle, giving the tide a lift.

A seahorse swings, in a barnacle swirl,
While anemones dance, giving it a twirl.
They sing of the days, when fishes would frolic,
And the ocean's humor stays ever symbolic.

Whispering Coral Castles

In a castle of coral, fish wear crowns,
Waving their fins with silly frowns.
A lobster's waltz, it's quite a scene,
Pinching crabs join in, a royal routine.

Starfish break dancing on the sea floor,
Shells tap their toes, wanting more.
A clam cracks jokes, making waves of cheer,
While octopuses juggle their lunch with a sneer.

A Dance of Sunlit Sands

On sunlit sands, the turtles glide,
Doing the cha-cha with stars as their guide.
A dolphin jumps high, a twist and a spin,
While sea urchins discuss the latest swim win.

Sand dollars gossip, they giggle and chatter,
"Hey, look at that crab, he's lost all his patter!"
With a flip and a flop, they all join the play,
A sandy fandango, brightening the day.

Undersea Melodies of Movement

A fishy chorus sings through the blue,
With clownfish cracking jokes, silly but true.
Seahorses stomp to a funky old beat,
While jellyfish sway with their gooey, soft feet.

The conch shells play sax, their tunes so bright,
And shrimps start to shuffle, just feeling right.
A playful pout from an eel as he sways,
While everyone laughs, in their own fishy ways.

Fins and Fragments of Dreams

In whimsical waters, dreams take a dive,
Fins flutter like flags, feeling so alive.
A squid with a top hat parades through the crowd,
While bubbles float up like dreams that are loud.

A flounder and flatfish host a big show,
Playing hide and seek, but they've nowhere to go.
With laughter and color, they twirl 'round the reef,
In the realm of the quirky, there's always belief.

Lament of the Sea Anemone

I sway and dance with every tide,
Holding tight to my crab, he won't slide.
But oh, the waves bring such silly games,
I just wanted peace, not fame for my names!

They tickle my tentacles, what a tease,
As fish swim by like they own the seas.
"Catch me if you can!" they giggle and dart,
While I just stay here, with style, not heart!

Currents of a Forgotten World

In a deep sea café, starfish sip on tea,
Whispering tales of fish history.
"I met a dolphin, sharp as a tack,
But he swam away, never looked back!"

Coral cocktails served on the rocks,
With glow-in-the-dark underwater clocks.
"Oh, remember the shark who just wouldn't quit?
He tried to dance, now he's lost his wit!"

The Colorful Parade of Life

Underneath the waves, it's quite a sight,
Fishes parade, make the ocean bright.
With sequins of scales and glittery tails,
They're swishing and swirling, with jests and wails!

Jellyfish juggle in the moon's soft glow,
While clowns of the sea put on quite the show.
Octopuses twirl with each graceful leg,
"I'm the best dancer!" they boast and beg!

Vibrations of a Brine-Kissed Dream

In my sleepy world, the seaweed does sway,
Jellybeans floating, they color my day.
The anchor's a pillow, I nap with glee,
While krill play chess, quite an unusual spree!

The winds whisper secrets to all of us here,
As barnacles belt out a brand-new cheer.
Shh, don't wake the octopus, he's dreaming big,
Planning a party, perhaps a sea jig!

A Tapestry of Fin and Flipper

A dolphin wore a hat so tall,
He said, "I'm here to have a ball!"
The fish all laughed, they swam around,
The best hat party underwater found.

A turtle tried to join the fun,
With shades on, looking like a bun.
They danced on shells, the laughter flew,
In ocean style, a wild zoo!

A crab with rhythm, clicked his claws,
In dance-off mode, he broke the laws.
"Don't pinch me, friend!" a flounder cried,
As all the creatures laughed and tried.

The octopus played tunes divine,
With ink as jet, he wished to shine.
But slipping on a slippery floor,
He squirted ink – now that's rapport!

The Breath of the Ocean Floor

A fish with hiccups started to sway,
His bubbles made the octopus say,
"Is that a song or just a burp?"
The clownfish laughed, doing the twerp.

A sea cucumber played the flute,
It looked like it was born to hoot.
A seahorse twirled with such great flair,
Then tangled up in seaweed hair.

A starfish sported dancey shoes,
With every step, it lost its blues.
But oh no! It slipped and fell quite hard,
As crabs erupted in applause, they marred!

The anemones clapped with glee,
As bubbles burst with every spree.
A giggling whale joined the choir,
And suddenly, the sea caught fire!

The Dance of the Seaweed

In a wavy world, where seaweed sways,
A kelp ballet took place for days.
A sea slug pirouetted so fine,
While saying, "I am the star, it's my time!"

The jellyfish glowed, led the parade,
With moves so smooth, they never fade.
The urchins laughed at such a sight,
As waves clapped in pure delight.

A fish in costume joined the scene,
Dressed as a pirate, all in green.
He tripped, he slipped, his treasure spilled,
A goldfish guffawed, oh how they thrilled!

The seaweed swayed in perfect tune,
A chorus of giggles beneath the moon.
Surfing on currents, they made their stand,
In the grandest dance of the ocean band!

Echoes of the Sunlit Depths

A crab with a megaphone so loud,
Took to the stage before the crowd.
"What did the fish say to the bait?"
Laughter erupted - it was quite the fate!

A parrotfish painted with flair,
Said, "I'm the Picasso of this lair!"
The angelfish posed for a selfie shot,
"Fish of the year? You know I've got!"

An eel in glasses, cool and spry,
Said, "Let's make waves, don't be shy!"
But tangled up in seaweed long,
He wriggled out with a silly song.

The sea felt like a circus now,
Fishes giggling, I'll take a bow.
Among the bubbles, laughter grew,
In the depths where sunshine broke through!

Brushstrokes of Salt and Sea

In a world where fish wear shoes,
And octopuses win at trivia clues,
The crab in a tux, oh what a sight,
He dances like no one's watching tonight.

The starfish tries its hand at art,
With colors that might just break your heart,
It splats paint all over the shore,
Leaving beachgoers laughing for more.

Seagulls join in for a grand ballet,
Twirling and flapping in a silly way,
While the blowfish tells a joke or two,
Making waves with laughter that feels so new.

As the sunset spills its hues,
Even the seaweed sings the blues,
In this salty place of endless fun,
The ocean's party has just begun!

A Canvas of Corals

Corals strut in polka dots,
The anemones pull hilarious pranks,
A parrotfish in a bowler hat,
Nibbles on a coral like a snack.

The painterfish mixes up the shade,
While clowns of the sea come out to parade,
A seahorse in platform shoes sways,
As they shimmy through the underwater bays.

Shrimp practice their tap dance routine,
While clownfish giggle, oh so keen,
The jellyfish twirl in slow-motion dance,
While everyone else gives them a chance.

So here on this vibrant ocean slate,
Laughter and bubbles seal their fate,
With colors and giggles all around,
Underwater fun is where it's found!

The Gentle Pull of the Deep

Down in the depths where the sun won't peek,
A whale does the limbo; the floor's just a creek,
   Octopus mimics a phone ringing loud,
Their antics get laughs from the curious crowd.

The turtles, they race, but they stop to snack,
'Swim slow,' says one, with a shell on its back,
A dolphin flips high, then lands with a splash,
   Telling fish jokes in a hurried dash.

Crabs throw a party with shells as their hats,
  While squids swirl spaghetti like acrobats,
They dance to the rhythm of ocean's delight,
  Making the deep a whimsical sight.

With laughter and glee in tidal embrace,
The sea's bottom hullabaloo takes its place,
Every shimmy and shake is a merry decree,
  Under the waves, let's be crazy and free!

The Sigh of the Undersea Garden

In the garden below where the sea cucumbers grow,
Live fish with no worries; they just steal the show,
Seahorses giggle, twirling with glee,
While sea urchins chuckle at their funny decree.

The seaweed is dancing; it sways to the beat,
Oysters tell tales of the seafood they meet,
Each rock is a canvas, so vibrant and bright,
Home to the mischief of shrimp at their flight.

Clams make up stories of treasures and pearls,
While the sand dollars laugh as the current unfurls,
A conch shell recites the most comical lore,
As the bubbles join in with a pop and a roar.

In this jolly patch of the salty embrace,
Each critter reflects a silly little face,
So dive deep, my friend; join the joyful brigade,
In the underwater garden, where laughter won't fade!

Prismatic Shadows on the Seafloor

In the ocean, colors play,
Dancing fish can steal the day.
Bubbles rise with giggles, too,
Seaweed sways like it's in a zoo.

Crabs in hats join in the fun,
Making mischief, on the run.
Starfish doing wiggly bends,
Underwater, laughter never ends.

Coral castles filled with cheer,
Tickle a porpoise, watch it steer.
Every wave brings silly sights,
Splashing joy on sunny nights.

Flowing Patterns of Nature's Art

A jellyfish floats, looking grand,
With tentacles that wave like hands.
Clownfish play hide and seek,
In a garden, oh so chic.

Seahorses prance, a waltz so fine,
Twisting around in a fishy line.
They giggle as they twirl and spin,
In this ocean, where do we begin?

Lobsters snap with crusty jokes,
While turtles tell of silly folks.
In nature's art, the laughter flows,
Creating smiles as the ocean glows.

Harmony in the Blue Expanse

Out in the deep, a grand parade,
Where sea anemones wave and trade.
Fish wear glasses, looking wise,
While dolphins dive to grab the prize.

A seagull tries its best to sing,
But fish outdo it, what a fling!
Harmonies from coral and shell,
Turn a beach to a grand hotel.

Octopuses paint with flair,
Filling the water with giggles in air.
An orchestra beneath the tide,
In this blue, we take a ride.

Cascading Patterns of Marine Grace

Bubble trails lead the way,
To a dance party where fish play.
A shrimp DJ spins the tunes,
While eels shake their silly looms.

Clown crabs stroll with swagger bold,
In the sea's funny tale retold.
Sea turtles groove, a sight to see,
Jellyfish wobbling so carefree.

Every splash, a giggle shared,
In this circus, no one's spared.
With each float, a surprising grace,
In the ocean's bright embrace.

Imprints in the Silty Abyss

In the mud, a crab did dance,
Wiggles and giggles, what a chance!
A fish in a tutu, quite the sight,
Chasing bubbles in the moonlight.

A starfish flipped, with flair and grace,
Doing cartwheels in this wild space.
With each little wave, they spark and shine,
Making the ocean feel just divine.

A sea cucumber, quite the bore,
Decided it's time to hit the shore.
But as it crawled, it sang a tune,
Wobbling like a silly balloon.

So gather 'round, let's laugh and play,
In the depths, we'll splash all day.
With quirky friends and silly charms,
Undersea, we'll find sweet calms.

Choreography of the Currents

A jellyfish wobbled, oh so bright,
Flapping its arms like it's in flight.
The fish swam past, gave quite a scare,
As two of them tangled in its hair!

The sea turtle joined, a slow-spin show,
With kids on the reef, putting on a glow.
They all tripped over sea urchins galore,
Good thing the tide left the door ajar!

A clownfish laughed at a shrimp's bad joke,
They giggled until their bubbles broke.
A mollusk passed, winked with flirtatious glee,
Dancing alone, 'come join' was the plea!

So come dive in, let the fun commence,
With silly friends, let's pile on the suspense.
In each wave, there's laughter that flows,
In the depths, the joy only grows!

Moonlit Hues of the Abyss

Bubbles rising, tickling the feet,
A squishy octopus can't find its seat.
It wore a green hat and striped blue socks,
Trying to dance on the coral blocks.

A parrotfish laughed, 'Look at that style!',
While making a sassy, colorful smile.
The sand dollar joined, with a twirl and spin,
Who knew that the ocean had such a grin?

A seashell chuckled, its secret revealed,
It once had a date, but it got unsealed.
"Never dates sandcastles," it said with a scoff,
"Those towers just crumble; it's better to scoff!"

So when the moon shines, let's all convene,
For the show in the waves is the best you've seen.
We'll dance like sea urchins, all joined in delight,
In the depths of the night, it feels just right!

The Secret Life of the Tide

The tide rolls in, a sneaky prank,
A clam pretended to be a tank.
With pearls and shells as its disguise,
It waved bye-bye to the seagull's cries.

A conch shell whispered some grand tales,
About fishy pirates and slippery snails.
They plotted a heist of a lost treasure chest,
And laughed together while taking a rest.

A dolphin's antics were video worthy,
As it flipped and flopped, looking real purty.
It told jokes to the unsuspecting fish,
"Oh don't be so crabby, just make a wish!"

So next time you peek at the ocean's glide,
Remember the fun of the shifting tide.
With creatures that giggle and swish all around,
In this watery dance, pure joy can be found!

Chronicles of the Colorful Deep

In a sea of blue, where the fish do prance,
A clownfish told jokes, giving all a chance.
The octopus juggled shells, a sight to behold,
While crabs tap danced, brave and bold.

A turtle named Larry wore sunglasses cool,
As he floated by, breaking every rule.
He said with a wink, "I'm just going for a ride!"
And waved to the dolphins, full of pride.

The seaweed swayed, in rhythm and rhyme,
As seahorses twirled, oh, what a time!
They formed a parade, all dressed up right,
Underwater disco, a shimmering night.

So if you dive down, don't forget to cheer,
For the jokes of the deep are what you'll hear!
Grab your snorkel and mask, jump in with glee,
Join the underwater fun, come dance with me!

The Lull of the Tide

The gentle waves hum a lullaby song,
While fish in their frocks boogie all day long.
A crab with a hat sells popcorn in shells,
While starfish audition for Broadway's finest tells.

A whale took a nap, snoring big and loud,
Scared away fish who had gathered a crowd.
They whispered and giggled, popping their fins,
Talking of adventures and all of their sins.

The sea cucumber dressed up in a gown,
Said, "Please don't look, I'm just a bit down!"
The jellyfish laughed, "Don't let it get you!
Let's dance!" and they twirled, like confetti in blue.

As the tide ebbs low, and the sun starts to set,
Every creature we'll see, will be hard to forget.
So next time you're near, don't forget your cheer,
For fun's always brewing when the tide's rolling near!

Sunsplash Over the Briny Deep

Oh the sun splashed bright over waters so clear,
Where fish wore their shades, laughing without fear.
A parrotfish painted, with colors so keen,
Said, "I'm an artist, the best you've seen!"

The pufferfish puffed, trying to show off,
But tripped on a seaweed, oh what a scoff!
He giggled and rolled, what a whimsical sight,
As the sea stars clapped, shining so bright.

A friendly old dolphin played leapfrog with me,
While sea turtles surfed on the waves with such glee.
They shouted and squealed, "What a wild ride!"
Jumping and splashing with carefree pride.

As the sun made its home in the purpley dusk,
Every fish twinkled, a fantastic husk.
So splash in the sea, let your spirit take flight,
In this watery world, where there's always delight.

Glimmers at the Water's Edge

At the edge of the sea, where the sand meets the foam,
Crabs play hide-and-seek, they're never alone.
With shells for their homes and sand for their beds,
They tell silly stories of fish and their heads.

A pelican swooped down, with a big, clumsy flap,
Landed right on a clam, oh, what a mishap!
The clam just laughed, "Hey, it's a fun little ride!
Next time, bring snacks, and I'll let you inside!"

Seagulls squawked loudly, with their beaks all aglow,
Though their plans were disrupted by a wave's cheeky flow.
They hopped and they flapped, caught in a game,
While the ocean just giggled, it wasn't to blame.

As day turns to night, and stars start to show,
Under the moonlight, the tide's dancing slow.
Join the edge of the water, let laughter be free,
For even the sea loves a silly jubilee!

Dance of the Undercurrent

In the sea's tricky waltz, fish start to twirl,
Seahorses jitterbug, giving finny whirl.
Crabs tap dance sideways, in a comical show,
Clams sing off-key, but we all love the flow.

An octopus spins with style, it looks quite slick,
While jellyfish bob, doing their own little trick.
A dolphin dives down, with a splash and a cheer,
"Catch me if you can!" it swims without fear.

Starfish lounge like pros, laid back on the sand,
Making sand angels with an arm of a hand.
Pufferfish giggle, we can hear their loud snickers,
As divers float by, they get quite the kickers.

The seaweed gets funky, it sways with a jig,
Anemones laugh, holding onto a gig.
With bubbles as beats, it's a wild ocean ball,
In this watery world, it's laughter for all.

Murmurs of the Ocean's Embrace

The waves whisper secrets in a bubbly tone,
Clownfish crack jokes, never swimming alone.
Coral giggles soft, in shades bright and bold,
Their colors are vibrant, like stories retold.

A turtle scans crowds with a curious grin,
While sea cucumbers just squirm from within.
"Don't mind me," says a shrimp, "I'm just here to snack,"
But the fish all laugh, "Don't you dare hold back!"

A school of bright angels, in a synchronized line,
Swirling and swaying, oh how they divine!
They bubble and gurgle as they play tag for fun,
Chasing their tails under the warming sun.

An eel pokes its head and shares a good pun,
"Why don't fish play piano? They get scales—just run!"
Laughter spreads wide, like the tide in the bay,
In this vibrant embrace, joy is here to stay.

Beneath the Surface: A Hidden Symphony

Deep down below, where the bubbles sing clear,
A symphony plays that the fish hold dear.
Clownfish conduct with their charming finesse,
While snapper on stage begins to impress.

The trumpetfish blow, creating a tune,
While seahorses sway, dancing 'neath the moon.
Guitarfish strum as the pufferfish hum,
Each note gets more laughable, oh what a drum!

An octopus winks, asking for a duet,
Two shrimp tap dance; it's a marvelous set.
A chorus of dolphins joins in with a cheer,
Their voices a melody, worth stopping to hear.

As bubbles ascend, carrying tales through the tide,
The kelp bends in rhythm, joining in with pride.
In this underwater gala, with jests never far,
The ocean's sweet laughter shines bright like a star.

Chasing Shades of Blue

In depths painted azure, where the silliness glows,
Fish chase their own shadows, where the sunlight flows.
"Got you!" calls a grouper with a giggling shout,
While the blues dance around, as they swish and twirl out.

Humor in currents, a flurry of sprites,
Swimming in circles, creating great heights.
A parrotfish yawns and says, "What a show!"
As jellyfish bubble up, putting on quite a glow.

Angelfish tease with a game of peek-a-boo,
As tangs race by, in a whirl of bright hue.
The hermit crabs chuckle, dragging shells with flair,
In the game of hide and seek, it's all a wild affair.

And when night falls, under the glowing moon,
The laughter still echoes, a light-hearted tune.
With shades of blue dancing, life's a vivid spree,
In underwater wonder, we're just happy to be.

A Diving Dreamscape

With fins that flap and bubbles rise,
I swam with fish wearing silly ties.
A turtle waved, a clownfish danced,
In this underwater party, I pranced.

Coral castles stood tall and bright,
An octopus in pajamas, what a sight!
Seashells giggled as I swam on by,
A dolphin tossed seaweed, oh my, oh my!

The sea anemones beckoned me near,
Whispering tales of mermaids and beer.
I dove through kelp with a graceful twist,
In this diving dream, how could I resist?

As waves tickled toes and laughter flowed,
I found my way through this wacky abode.
For in the depths where the silliness thrives,
The ocean sings joy, in every dive!

Tide's Rhythmic Lullaby

The ocean hums a cheeky tune,
Surfboards dance, the sun's a boon.
Seagulls squawked in a comic choir,
While beach balls rolled like a merry tire.

Crabs in costumes, strutting their claws,
Winking at people with silly jaws.
The tide's embrace, a soft embrace,
Turns every frown into a smiling face.

As I surfed a wave shaped like a cow,
I took a plunge and lost my brow.
The water splashed, fish laughed with cheer,
What a splendiferous day, oh dear!

Now every wave whispers a jest,
In the heart of the tide, we're truly blessed.
So join the fun where the waters sway,
For life's a beach, let the good times play!

The Words of the Wind and Water

The breeze giggled, tickling my toes,
While windsurfing past a dolphin in clothes.
He winked at me with a toothy grin,
"Let's race!" he shouted, "I'll surely win!"

A pelican named Pete dropped a fish,
I caught it with laughter, what a dish!
The waves whispered secrets, oh yes indeed,
To every passing boat, they gave a breed.

Seashells conspired, plotting in rhyme,
"Let's make some mischief, now's our prime!"
A crab in a hat joined the swell,
Chanting funny verses, casting a spell.

So let's gather 'round where the water plays,
Listening closely to the ocean's ways.
For in this world of frolic and fun,
Each splash is a story, a dance that's begun!

Soft Caresses of the Surf

The surf tickled my feet with such delight,
As waves rolled in with a gentle bite.
I built a castle, but it tumbled down,
A sea star giggled, wearing a crown.

Mermaids sang while brushing their hair,
With seashell combs, they floated with flair.
A whale popped up, struck a pose just right,
"Swim with me, for it's a funny sight!"

The ocean's arms wrapped me tight,
As crabs cheered on with all their might.
Each wave told jokes that cracked the sand,
Creating laughter across the land.

So splash in the surf, let worries go,
You never know where the tide may flow.
For in this watery world of glee,
Each wave is a laugh, come join me, whee!

Echoes in the Tides

In the ocean's grand ballet,
Fish wear silly hats all day.
Crabs dance cha-cha in the sand,
Twirling shells, they'll make a band.

Seagulls swoop to snatch a fry,
While dolphins leap and laugh on high.
A starfish plays the ukulele,
Singing tunes quite jazzy, maybe!

Jellyfish float with flair and grace,
Sticky notes, they leave in space.
Octopuses twirl in pure delight,
Winking at the moon each night.

So join this party, what a sight,
Underwater disco, pure delight!
With bubbles popping, laughter's spread,
In the waves, we'll dance instead!

Shimmering Depths of Serenity

A turtle twirls in a polka dot suit,
Chasing bubbles, oh how cute!
Clams chuckle, shutter their shells,
Holding secrets, oh how it dwells.

A fish with glasses, reading a book,
Gives wise advice, just take a look.
Seahorses giggle, their tails entwined,
Creating chaos, not one left behind.

The coral reefs host a tea party sweet,
With seaweed treats no one could beat.
Starfish serve, all in a whirl,
While seashells spin and slightly twirl.

But watch out for the sneaky eel,
He plays tricks that are truly surreal!
With a wink and a dance, he slips away,
Leaving the fish in a fray.

Secrets Beneath the Waves

Down below, where the funny fish roam,
A pufferfish dreams of a cozy home.
With balloons tied, they dance and glide,
In fashionable bubbles, they take pride.

An anemone plays peek-a-boo,
While clownfish dodge like they always do.
The sea cucumbers gossip and sway,
Sharing tales of their wild day.

Scallops wear jewelry, shimmering bright,
Their glittery shells, pure fashion delight.
With pearls of wisdom, they chirp and cheer,
As sardines spin in a synchronized leer.

The jellyfish gather for a group fit,
Doing aerobics, not one bit legit!
With a squish and a splash, they sway so bold,
Underwater antics, a sight to behold!

Currents of Colorful Life

The parrotfish paints the ocean floor,
Colors that dazzle, we all adore.
A sideways crab brings the silly jokes,
While starry night fish share silly pokes.

Underwater, the laughter flows,
Every wave brings new silly shows.
A group of snails in a tug-of-war,
Who knew slowpokes could go so far?

The annoying gulls steal a fry or two,
While the catfish strut in their fancy shoe.
Seahorses boast of their swirly tails,
Telling tales of their colorful trails.

In this magical world, all things align,
Each splash a giggle, so divine!
So swim along, join the goofy spree,
In the depths where we all can be free!

Life's Interlude Amongst the Currents.

Fish in tuxedos, swimming so fine,
They twirl and they tango, oh how they shine!
Crabs dance with rhythm, claws held so high,
While seaweed sways gently, like it's shy.

A dolphin stands up, takes a bow on the edge,
With friends all around, it's quite the pledge!
The starfish in glitter won't let it go,
Shouting 'Look at me!' from below.

A octopus juggling with flair and with style,
A sea cucumber yawns, "Can you stay for a while?"
Pufferfish snicker, as bubbles they blow,
While the sand dollars giggle, 'Oh, what a show!'

With currents of laughter, the seafloor's alive,
Where each kooky creature knows how to thrive!
In an underwater circus, our antics abound,
Life here is wacky, come on, gather 'round!

Whispers of the Coral Tide

Anemones wiggle in a colorful dance,
Clownfish pop out, taking a chance.
With winks and with grins, they play hide and seek,
In the sea's funny game, it's the best kind of week.

Sea horses laughing, their tails all entwine,
While jellyfish giggle, 'We're feeling divine!'
A grouper in glasses, a real looking scholar,
Accidentally trips, and oh, what a holler!

A tiny shrimp joking, 'I'm tougher than you!'
While mollusks just chuckle, 'We've got a crew!'
With a slow, steady wave, a turtle gives pause,
To admire the others' lovely sea laws.

Amongst colors so vivid, a party takes flight,
Underwater shenanigans fill up the night.
Laughter and bubbles dance in the light,
In this world of the silly, oh what a sight!

Echoes Beneath the Waves

With sea stars that giggle and swim through the gloom,
The hermit crabs waltz, making shells their own room.
A whale sings a note that's hilariously flat,
The fishes all gather and laugh, 'Oh, what's that?'

In schools, all the fish share their combs and their brushes,

While moon jellies glide, making soft, squishy hushes.
Clownfish tell tales; each one is a jest,
Of pirates who never managed the quest!

The friendly sea turtle hums while he drifts,
With laughter that twinkles, he shares all his gifts.
A treasure chest open, with pearls far and wide,
But it's full of seaweed – what a fun ride!

In the currents they flutter, embracing the jest,
With giggles and gurgles, they live their best quest.
For under the surface, where echoes are found,
Life's a funny tale that goes round and round!

Secrets of the Silent Lagoon

In the tranquil lagoon, the fish play in jest,
With secrets and laughter, they feel so blessed.
A grouchy old turtle, just trying to nap,
Gets pinched by a crab, what a slip of the flap!

The mermaids are giggling, their hair in a mess,
As they play 'Four Lost Shoes' in the coral dress.
Each scallop takes turns, they decide on a tale,
Of treasures and pirates that always seem pale.

The sea otters frolic, with rocks in their paws,
Cracking up shells while forgetting the cause.
Each splash and each turn brings goofy delight,
In the silent oasis, it's all very bright!

So here in the calm, there's nothing to fear,
With laughter that bubbles, let's spread some cheer!
Amongst all the colors and stories so grand,
Life swims with humor in this funny land!

Harmony among the Sea Fans

In the depths, the sea fans swayed,
Dancing round like they just made a trade.
The clownfish giggled, their faces so bright,
Twirling and swirling—oh, what a sight!

A starfish chuckled, skin so bumpy,
He joked with a crab, who looked a bit grumpy.
"Why don't you dance? Come join the cheer!"
The crab just sighed, "I've two left feet, dear."

Anemones wiggled, no sense of shame,
Playing dress-up; oh, what a game!
The sea turtles rolled their eyes with glee,
"Water ballet? We'd win the marquee!"

So in the blue, the laughter grew loud,
As sea fans fluttered, so merry and proud.
Every wave brought a chuckle or two,
Underwater giggles: a party so true!

Life's Swaying Serenade

In the ocean's cradle, the seaweed waves,
Sings a tune that the seahorse braves.
With tiny top hats, they jiggle with flair,
A dance-off begins; it's hard to compare!

The pufferfish puffs in a spontaneous beat,
While parrotfish snicker on their colorful seat.
"I'm the best dancer!" the puffer declares,
But a jellyfish floats in without any cares.

They frolic and flounce, the creatures so spry,
In bubbles of laughter as the currents fly by.
An octopus shows off its eight-armed twist,
The crowd goes wild, it's too good to miss!

So join the fun where the sunbeams gleam,
Life's a grand dance, or so it would seem.
In the ocean's embrace, they twirl and they sway,
Creating new songs as they play through the day!

Shadows of the Tide Pools

In tide pools where shadows play hide and seek,
A crab wears a hat made from sea-sponge chic.
Hermit crabs grumble, they lift and they bump,
"Whose shell is this? It makes me feel plump!"

Starfish eavesdrop, their limbs all aglow,
Giggling softly as wiggly things flow.
A sea cucumber slips on a slick rock,
"This slippery dance is a real shock!"

The anemones laugh, tickled by waves,
As snails wind around with their armored knaves.
"Don't fret about fashion, everybody's fab!"
Said a wise old oyster with a fabulous gab.

In the shadows where secrets are shared,
Laughter and friendship, the riches we've bared.
So explore the tide pools where whimsy is found,
Where silliness flourishes and joy knows no bounds!

Beneath the Shell's Whisper

Underneath shells, a committee convenes,
With squints and gossip, they share all their means.
A scallop chimes in, with pearls of delight,
"Who dived for dinner last Friday night?"

A clam giggles back, ``Just so you know,
I had my eye on the gourmet" in slow!
But sushi was served; I took my first bite,
And now I'm just shell-shocked with fright!"

A sea snail chuckles, feeling quite spry,
"I may be slow, but watch me fly high!
With my flavorful tales, I'm your local bard,
But lately, I'm feeling a bit off-guard!"

So beneath the shells, those whispers so bright,
Reveal all the shenanigans under moonlight.
As laughter echoes through waters so blue,
Life underwater, a comedy too!

Shadows in the Seagrass

Bobby the crab wore his best suit,
Dancing in seagrass, oh what a brute!
Fish laughed aloud, with scales all aglow,
As Bobby tripped over a sea cucumber's toe.

A turtle joined in, just to impress,
Wobbling along in a bright, frilly dress.
They twirled and they whirled, like a dizzying parade,
Only to stop when the seahorses played.

The jellyfish giggled, so jelly and bright,
They bounced to the beats of a fishy delight.
And as shadows danced, in the warm ocean bed,
Bobby yelled, "Who's next? Come dance on my head!"

So remember this tale when you're splashing around,
In the sea, where the laughter and fun can be found.
For these underwater shenanigans, oh what a spree,
Just look out for Bobby, he's still on the spree!

Tides of Transience

Once a clownfish named Lou had a flair,
He wore tiny glasses, styled with care.
His friends laughed and teased, said, "What's the show?"
But Lou just winked, with a confident glow.

The ocean's a stage, with waves acting bold,
Where corals are gossiping, secrets unfold.
Fish hurry by with a comedic rush,
As a starfish said, "I'm not one for a crush!"

When tides retreat, the sea cucumbers hide,
"I'm just a soft pillow, come take a ride!"
Laughter ensued, through barnacle lanes,
With seaweed that swayed, making silly gains.

So next time you're down by the water's bright side,
Join in the fun, take laughter for a ride.
The tide might change, like jokes on a reel,
But the giggles and grins, that's the real deal!

The Symphony of Color and Shadow

A trumpetfish played a jazzy old tune,
While a grouper danced under the glowing moon.
"Keep up, you slowpoke!" the wrasse shouted loud,
As the octopus jammed, feeling great and proud.

Coral reefs swayed, a wild, vibrant scene,
With colors that sparkled, oh, what a machine!
The parrotfish croaked, in a voice full of glee,
"Let's break out the party, swim wild and free!"

The sea urchins above were tapping their spines,
Creating a rhythm with style that aligns.
While the dories formed lines, to show off their flair,
Looking sharp in their suits, like they just didn't care.

So if you dive deep, amidst shadows and light,
Expect laughter and music, what a grand sight!
In this joyful ballet of fishy delight,
Every move is a note, every splash feels just right!

The Hidden Rhythm of the Reef

In the coral crannies, a treasure was found,
A disco ball left by a mermaid, how profound!
The clams clapped their shells, keeping up with the tune,
While shrimp served snacks, singing, "Join us at noon!"

A flounder was grooving, flat on the floor,
"Don't judge my moves, I'm a fish, not a bore!"
The eels on the sidelines were giving advice,
"Just wiggle and flaunt, don't think twice!"

With bubbles and giggles, the night came alive,
As the underwater crew learned how to jive.
It was a raucous affair, filled with sea-faring cheer,
Where even the shy fish felt happy to steer!

So if you ever find that hidden cove,
With a dance party happening, consider yourself strove.
For laughter is boundless, in the sea's great embrace,
Dive in and find joy, in this watery space!

Mysteries of the Marine Ballet

With fins that flutter, fish do prance,
Like tiny dancers in a chance.
A crab steals steps, oh what a show,
He tangoes sideways, all aglow.

Stars of the sea, they twirl and leap,
As seaweed sways, a secret keep.
A clownfish grins, a jester true,
In this grand ball, he steals the view.

The octopus, a master of disguise,
Waltzes through with clever lies.
He flips and flops with eight-armed flair,
A choreographed underwater affair.

But watch your step, watch your toes!
The seahorse trips, and over he goes.
With giggles shared, they start anew,
In the marine ballet, a comical crew.

Underwater Sunbeams

Sunbeams dance in playful delight,
Tickling fish with golden light.
The jellyfish floats, a party hat,
While dolphins splash, 'How about that!'

A treasure chest, just for show,
Filled with shells and bubbles aglow.
The clownfish laughs, 'What a find!'
As sea stars stretch, a bit unwind.

Coral reefs, a colorful sight,
Like candy land, oh what a bite!
The angelfish twirls, in colors bold,
Showing off like a pot of gold.

But wait, who's that hiding quite near?
A crab playing peek-a-boo, oh dear!
With all the laughs under the sea,
Sunbeams shine in pure glee.

Celestial Tides and Teeming Schools

In schools they come, bright fish parade,
Flipping and flopping, they're not afraid.
A guppy shouts, 'Let's race for fun!'
While lurking shadows groan, 'Oh, run!'

Moonlit tides twinkle, oh so bright,
Pufferfish puffing, what a sight!
They giggle through bubbles, float like a dream,
This underwater world, a sparkling gleam.

Squids in a circle, making a plan,
'Let's host a party, here's our clan!'
With sea cucumbers as the quirky band,
The ocean floor shakes, all perfectly planned.

But hold on tight, here comes a whirl,
A turtle spins, giving a twirl.
With laughter echoing in salty air,
At celestial tides, we have found our flair.

The Lure of the Twilight Waters

Twilight whispers, shadows grow,
Anemones giggle, waving a hello.
The hermit crab dons shells like hats,
While snails crawl slow, sharing chit-chats.

The fish shout jokes, oh what a jest,
"Why did the seaweed never rest?"
They tickle the tails, and giggles float,
In twilight's calm, laughter's the boat.

A sea turtle slides, oh, look at him glide,
He carries the moonlight on his back with pride.
'Let's race to the coral, who's in the lead?'
And dolphins dart forth like they've taken heed.

In the twilight's embrace, fun takes the stage,
With fishy antics, oh, they engage.
The waters shimmer with joy and cheer,
In the twilight glow, all play's sincere.

Stories Written in Sand and Sea

A crab wearing shades strolls on the shore,
A seagull swoops down, then steals his decor.
The tides tell tales, of treasures and dread,
While flip-flops float by, with laughter, they tread.

The starfish sings songs about lost sailor's socks,
While dolphins do ballet on barnacled rocks.
In a castle of sand, a young child proclaims,
"My kingdom is mighty! Though it melts with the rain!"

A fish in a tuxedo, quite dapper and neat,
Invites all the crabs for a fine cocktail meet.
They toast with seaweed and sip from a shell,
While jellyfish bob to the rhythm so swell.

And as the sun sets, the stories unwind,
Of goofy adventures, silliness combined.
So heed the good waves, as they whisper and sway,
For laughter is found where the ocean holds sway.

The Enchantment of the Hydroplane

A toddler on a floatie wants to take off,
Sailing through puddles with a giggly scoff.
The plane zooms above, honking 'honk-honk!'
As waves leap and dance, turning fish into bonk!

An octopus pilot adjusts his bright hat,
While on the radio, a crab plays the cat.
It's a rock and roll party for all on the bay,
As seagulls throw confetti, in their awkward display.

The waves make a splash as they try to keep cool,
While shells play fetch with a very wet pool.
The fish in the cockpit wear goggles and grin,
As the plane does a loop—whoops! Let's do that again!

A gull takes a selfie, yes, that's quite the sight,
With a laugh and a squawk, they capture the flight.
And under the moon, as the laughter takes flight,
Even fish in their car can't think of a fright.

Waves of Serendipity

A wave rolled its way with a twist and a shout,
Bumping a whale who said, "What's this about?"
With a splash and a giggle, they started a race,
Dodging floating pineapples, it's quite the place!

The clams play cards, they call it 'Shell Poker',
While fish in a school share jokes with a joker.
The tides keep the secrets, the surf gets quite wild,
As a crab conducts concerts for every sea child.

What's that on the beach? A lost rubber duck,
He's looking for friends—oh, what a good luck!
A treasure map drawn on a seaweed scroll,
Leads to an ice cream truck—oh, that's how they roll!

So when life is swirling, don't fret and fume,
Just dive in the sea for a chance to zoom.
With laughter and joy in the dance of the foam,
You'll find every giggle leads straight to your home.

Colors that Sing Beneath

In a coral fiesta with colors so bright,
A clam plays the trumpet, what a funny sight!
Gobies are dancing in their disco ball shoes,
While parrotfish paint with a rainbow of hues.

The seaweed in rhythm sways side to side,
As a fish in a tutu becomes the great guide.
With bubbles for energy, they float through the blue,
Transforming each moment to an art debut.

A conch shell records every laugh from the crowd,
While turtles are chillin', they've taken a bow.
The laughter cascades like a sweet ocean breeze,
And all the bright colors bring joy to the seas.

So if you're feeling dull when the sun starts to set,
Just dive in the waters, don't have any regret.
For beneath the soft surface where the giggles are free,
Colors come alive, just come dance with me!

A Poem of Surging Seascapes

The fish wear hats, it's quite the sight,
As they dance in schools, left and right.
A crab walks sideways, a comical strut,
While a sea turtle gives a playful tut.

The jellyfish jiggle in a wobbly way,
Chasing the bubbles that float and sway.
An octopus tries to do a little spin,
But ends up tangled, oh, where to begin?

Seashells gossip, they have their say,
About the dolphins, how they love to play.
A clownfish cracks jokes in a bright anemone,
"Stop swimming in circles, you're making me dizzy!"

With every wave that crashes near,
The ocean chuckles, it's full of cheer.
Under the surface, a party awaits,
In the realm of coral, undersea fates.

The Immutable Pulse of the Ocean

The waves hum tunes, a rhythmic beat,
As seagulls perform their aerial feat.
A starfish argues with a stubborn snail,
"Why crawl so slow? Come join the trail!"

A whale tells tales from the depths so deep,
While tiny shrimp giggle and leap.
And a grouper grumbles 'bout his lost sock,
While the clownfish laugh, oh, what a shock!

The seaweed dances, like it's got moves,
Making mermaids groan, as they lose their grooves.
A dolphin flips, trying hard to impress,
While a pufferfish pouts, feeling the stress.

The current giggles, whispering light,
As the ocean sparkles, a dazzling sight.
So step in the water, take off your shoes,
Join the splash party, you've got nothing to lose!

Daughters of the Shallows

In the shallows, where laughter flows,
Mermaids trade secrets, nobody knows.
A clam rolls its eyes at a fishy pun,
While a crab declares, "This day is fun!"

Starfish play games, go catch the tide,
With a sea cucumber as their guide.
A pet hermit crab boasts a splendid shell,
Taking first place, oh, isn't it swell?

Seahorses twirl, a little ballet,
Tickling the sunbeams that come out to play.
While a stingray drags in a sandcastle lost,
"Who built this?" it wonders, but laughs at the cost.

In the shallow waters, glee can be found,
As fish serenade with a bubbling sound.
So dive in, my friend, find joy in the seas,
Where every splash brings a giggle with ease!

The Hidden Harmony of the Waters

Bubbles rise like notes from a song,
As the fish hum along, it won't take long.
A deep-sea creature croons a low bass,
While a flatfish fakes it, just playing face.

Anemones sway, guiding lost fish,
"Hey buddy, come here, we got a wish!"
But the blowfish puffs, as if on cue,
"Remember, my friends, I can't swim too!"

A rogue wave wobbles, but it can't hide,
The laughter echoing from the tide.
A sea cucumber's punchline is key,
"Why be a star when you can be sea?"

So splash in the blues, let your worries flee,
The sea's a jester, come dance with glee.
In the hidden spots where harmony glows,
You'll find the fun that the ocean bestows.

Underwater Gardens of Delight

Bubbles dance in laughter bright,
Seaweed sways, what a sight!
A crab in a top hat prances by,
While fish in tuxedos twirl and fly.

Jellyfish wear hats made of cheese,
Snails on scooters, cruising with ease.
A conch shell orchestra plays a tune,
As seahorses waltz beneath the moon.

Corals giggle, tickled by the tide,
An octopus with flair, full of pride.
Lobsters in shades, they're out to impress,
In this underwater party, nothing's a mess!

A dazzling dance, the sea breaks out,
With laughter and fun, there's never a doubt.
Underwater gardens, a joyful parade,
With all the surprises that nature has made.

A Symphony of Seafoam and Starfish

Starfish strum on seashell guitars,
While sea cucumbers play the bazaar.
Turtles tap dance on coral stage,
As laughter erupts like a bubbly rage.

The seafoam giggles, a frothy delight,
Pufferfish puffing, trying to take flight.
A slippery eel slips on a shoe,
While clownfish crack jokes, what a crew!

The dolphins dive, they flip and they swirl,
As mermaids join in, giving it a whirl.
What a ruckus, this magical show,
Underwater freedom, come on, let's go!

With bubbles of laughter, the ocean sings,
In the symphony of life, joy always clings.
Bright colors abound, how silly they play,
A party in the sea, hip-hip-hooray!

Lost Treasures of the Amplified Ocean

Goldfish wearing crowns, oh what a sight,
Searching for treasures that twinkle so bright.
A crab with a map that's oddly drawn,
He shrugs and he scuttles, 'I'll find it by dawn!'

Clams gossip about where the riches may be,
While clowns in their wigs swim about with glee.
A sunken ship filled with rubber ducks,
Makes a floating playground, oh, how it plucks!

The barnacles chat, they're having a ball,
As octopuses juggle, not dropping a thing at all.
Bubbles of laughter, oh what a pain,
Finding lost treasures in this silly domain!

Through the jellyfish fields, they giggle and swim,
In search of their glories, chances not grim.
The ocean's a mystery, a treasure trove wide,
Where hilarity thrives, and secrets abide!

Kaleidoscope of the Abyss

In the colorful depths, where the silly fish play,
A disco ball shines in a glittering way.
Lobsters in tutus, they twirl all around,
Spreading joy, oh what a fabulous sound!

Anemones bounce to a bubbly beat,
While plankton compete for a dance-off seat.
So many colors, a vibrant delight,
This cozy abyss is a wondrous sight!

Grouper in shades thinks he's quite the star,
While sardines giggle from a nearby jar.
The depths hold surprises in every nook,
With comedy and chaos in every book!

As laughter erupts from sea creatures galore,
The kaleidoscope spins, we laugh even more.
Life in the ocean, a whimsical spree,
Where the depths are alive with pure comedy!

A Legacy of Blue

In the depths where fish wear crowns,
A clown with style rarely frowns.
He juggles shells, a sight to see,
While shrimp stomp dance, oh what glee!

A lobster struts with head held high,
Pretends to be a sea-faring guy.
But in his claws, he holds a snack,
With every step, a crunchy crack!

The turtle twirls in a goofy way,
Wearing sunglasses, bright as day.
While seahorses giggle and glide,
In this world where quirks collide!

With waves that tickle, life's a blast,
In the oceans, fun is unsurpassed!
Each story told will weave and spin,
A legacy of laughs, let's begin!

The Grace of the Ocean's Ballad

The jellyfish sway like dancers bold,
With tentacles shimmering, gold to behold.
They twirl with grace in a slimy ballet,
Making fish giggle, 'Hey, look at them play!'

With sea urchins posing like superstars,
They challenge the waves and shoot out their spurs.
While crabs do the cha-cha on sandy floor,
Saying, 'Join us now, we won't keep score!'

A dolphin jumps in a somersault whirl,
While fish cheer along, giving a twirl.
They sing loud songs, funny and bright,
Creating a symphony of sheer delight!

In the ocean's embrace, laughter awakes,
With the quirkiest friends who make no mistakes!
A ballad of joy in every wave's crest,
In this watery world, we're truly blessed!

The Sea's Canvas Unfurled

On the seabed, colors burst free,
As fish play tag in harmony.
A starfish winks with a cheeky grin,
While anemones sway like they've got a twin!

A parrotfish paints with vibrant hues,
While corals gossip about sea news.
The octopus chuckles, brushes in hand,
Creating wacky art, oh so grand!

With every swirl and every splash,
The creatures laugh, in a joyful dash.
An angelfish flaunts its dazzling attire,
Spreading the cheer like it's on fire!

From the depths to the shores, the fun is vast,
In a world where goofy friendships are cast.
A canvas alive with laughter and cheer,
In the heart of the sea, we hold dear!

Richness Beneath the Surface

Beneath the waves, a treasure trove,
With a clam that thinks it's a stoic grove.
While snails debate who's the fastest of all,
In a race for a cracker—who'll take the fall?

A pufferfish puffs, trying to look cool,
But forgets it's a game; what a fool!
With bubbles galore, he floats like a balloon,
Dancing with laughter to a jubilant tune!

A group of fish plays hide and seek,
While the sea cucumber just feels bleak.
He shimmies slow, yet dreams of the day,
When he too can join in and frolic and play!

In the depths, where silliness reigns,
Life's richest moments break all the chains.
With laughter beneath every crest and curl,
The sea's bounty shines, what a funny world!

www.ingramcontent.com/pod-product-compliance
Lightning Source LLC
Chambersburg PA
CBHW062113280426
43661CB00086B/594